5

LET'S GO

4th Edition

WORKBOOK

Ritsuko Nakata

Karen Frazier

Barbara Hoskins

Penny Laporte

OXFORD

UNIVERSITY PRESS

Let's Talk

A Read and write.

| We don't have enough. | I think so. | See you soon! | How many do we need? |

1. **Is everything ready for the party? Are there enough pretzels?**

   _____.
   There are three bags.

2. **How many cans of soda are there?**

   There is only one can.
   _____.

3. _____?

   We need twelve cans.

   OK. _____!

B Match and write.

a can	cans	a bag	bags
a bottle	bottles	a piece	pieces

1.

2.

3.

4.

5.

6.

7.

8.

- _____ tomatoes
- _pieces of_ watermelon
- _____ pizza
- _____ soda
- _____ potato chips
- _____ beans
- _____ pretzels
- _____ water

C Look at B. Answer the question.

How many are there?

1. There are _two pieces of watermelon._____

2. There is _one_____.

3. _____.

4. _____.

5. _____.

6. _____.

7. _____.

8. _____.

Let's Learn

A Look and write.

1.  a lot of nuts

2.  _____

3. _____

4. _____

5. _____

6. _____

7.  _____

8. _____

B Look, read, and check.

1.

Are there a lot of cookies?
- ☐ Yes, there are.
- ☐ No, there aren't.

2.

Are there a lot of sandwiches?
- ☐ Yes, there are.
- ☐ No, there aren't.

3.

Are there a lot of hot dogs?
- ☐ Yes, there are.
- ☐ No, there aren't.

4.

Are there a lot of cupcakes?
- ☐ Yes, there are.
- ☐ No, there aren't.

C Look, read, and circle.

1.

There are   a few / a lot of   blueberries.

2.

There are   a few / a lot of   nuts.

3.

There are   a few / a lot of   cherries.

4.

There are   a few / a lot of   cans of soda.

D Write the questions and answers.

1. How many cherries are there?

   There are a few cherries.

2. How many blueberries are there?

   _____.

3. How many bottles are there?

   _____ bottles.

4. How many cookies are there?

   _____.

5. _____?

   There are a lot.

6. _____?

   There are a few.

Let's Learn More

A Match.

1. There is a little pudding. •

2. There is a lot of lemonade. •

3. There is a lot of cheese. •

4. There is a little pie. •

5. There is a lot of popcorn. •

6. There is a little water. •

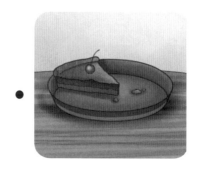

B Look and write.

1.

_____ pie.

2.

_____ fruit.

C Write the questions and answers.

> a lot of   a little   a few   How many   How much

1.

How much fruit is there?
There is a lot of fruit.

2.

How many _____ ?
There are _____ pretzels.

3.

_____ ?
_____ .

4.

_____ ?
_____ .

5.

_____ ?
_____ .

6.

_____ ?
_____ potato chips.

Let's Read

A Read and write.

| bones | dinosaurs | meat | millions | plants | scientists |

DINOSAURS

Dinosaurs lived _____ of years ago. There were a lot of _____ then. What did they eat? Did they buy bags of dinosaur food? Did they eat pieces of bread? No!

Scientists studied bones, too. Many dinosaurs had big, long _____. They were tall. They could reach the leaves on trees, but they couldn't jump. Some dinosaurs had little, short bones. They could climb trees.

Scientists studied dinosaur teeth. The _____ learned many things. For example, many dinosaurs ate _____. Some dinosaurs ate _____.

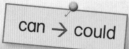

can → could

B Answer the questions.

1. Were there stores millions of years ago?

_____.

2. Did dinosaurs buy bags of dinosaur food?

_____.

3. Who studied dinosaur teeth?

_____

4. What did they learn from dinosaur teeth?

_____.

5. What could taller dinosaurs do?

_____

C Read and number the pictures.

1. Many dinosaurs ate meat.
3. They could climb trees.

2. They could reach the leaves on trees.
4. Some dinosaurs had little, short bones.

D What about you? Answer the questions.

1. What do you eat? _____

_____.

2. Can you climb trees? _____

_____.

3. Are you taller or shorter than your friends? _____

_____.

Unit 2 Comparing Animals

Let's Talk

A Read and check.

1. A zebra is slower than a gazelle.
   Really? That's interesting.

2. Wow! Look at that cat! It's as fast as a polar bear!
   That's interesting.

3. A man is faster than a skunk!
   Are you sure?
   Yes, I'm sure. Look!

B Look and write.

Yes, I'm sure.　　No, I'm not sure.

Are you sure?

_____.

_____.

4+4=9

C Complete the questions and answers.

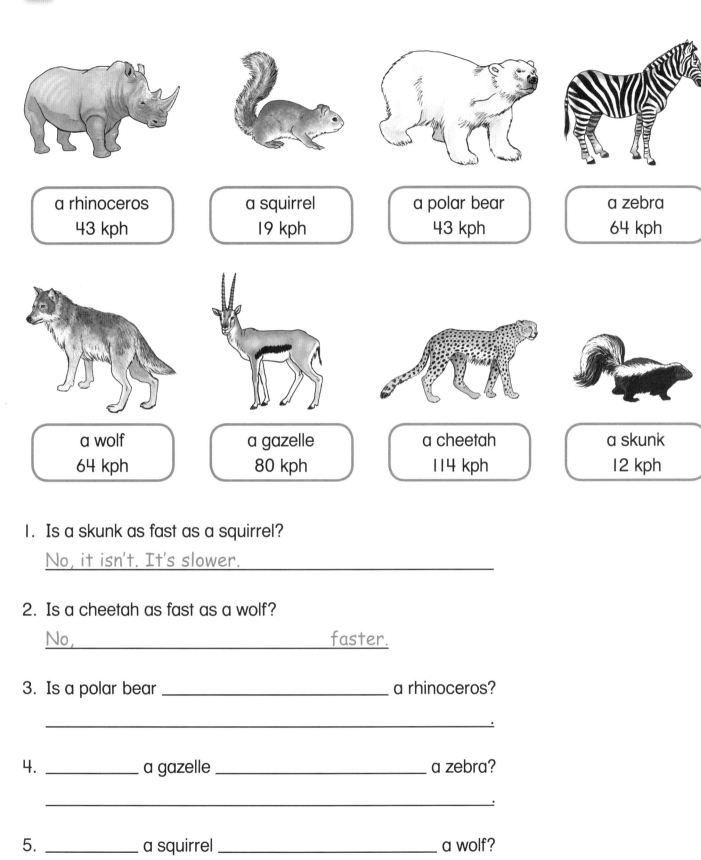

| a rhinoceros 43 kph | a squirrel 19 kph | a polar bear 43 kph | a zebra 64 kph |
| a wolf 64 kph | a gazelle 80 kph | a cheetah 114 kph | a skunk 12 kph |

1. Is a skunk as fast as a squirrel?

   No, it isn't. It's slower. _____

2. Is a cheetah as fast as a wolf?

   No, _____ faster.

3. Is a polar bear _____ a rhinoceros?

   _____.

4. _____ a gazelle _____ a zebra?

   _____.

5. _____ a squirrel _____ a wolf?

   _____.

Let's Learn

A Write the questions and answers.

elephant   squirrel   airplane   car

1. Which one is larger?

The elephant is larger. _____

2. Which one is faster?

_____.

rhinoceros   turtle   polar bear   skunk

3. Which one is slower?

_____.

4. Which one is smaller?

_____.

zebra   gazelle   skateboard   bicycle

5. _____?

The zebra is slower. _____

6. _____?

_____ faster.

B Look and write.

(airplane)

(car)

(bicycle)

1. Which one is the fastest?

   The airplane is the fastest.

2. Which one is the largest?

   _____.

3. Which one is the slowest?

   _____.

4. Which one is the smallest?

   _____.

C Unscramble and match.

1. one the slowest is Which?

   _____ ?

2. smallest Which the one is?

   _____ ?

3. Which fastest the is one?

   _____ ?

4. is largest Which one the?

   _____ ?

Let's Learn More

A Unscramble and write.

1. cilidesou

   <u>de</u> _____

2. cruleagf

   _____

3. spexeveni

   _____

4. fourcoll

   _____

B Write the questions and answers.

1. Which one is more delicious?

   <u>The cake is more delicious.</u> _____

2. Which one is less delicious?

   _____.

3. _____?

   <u>The cupcake is more delicious.</u> _____

4. _____?

   <u>The cake is less delicious.</u> _____

C Unscramble and write.

1. turtle / least / is / the / The / expensive

   _____.

2. The / most / bird / colorful / is / the

   _____.

3. is / the / cat / most / The / graceful

   _____.

D Answer the questions.

1. Which one is the most colorful?

   The _____.

   Is the squirrel less colorful than
   the fish?

   _____.

2. Which one is the least graceful?

   _____.

   Is the frog more graceful than
   the gazelle?

   _____.

Let's Read

A Read and write.

backward	hummingbird	mimic octopus	stronger
change	jellyfish		stripes

Did You Know?
Read some of the most interesting things about animals.

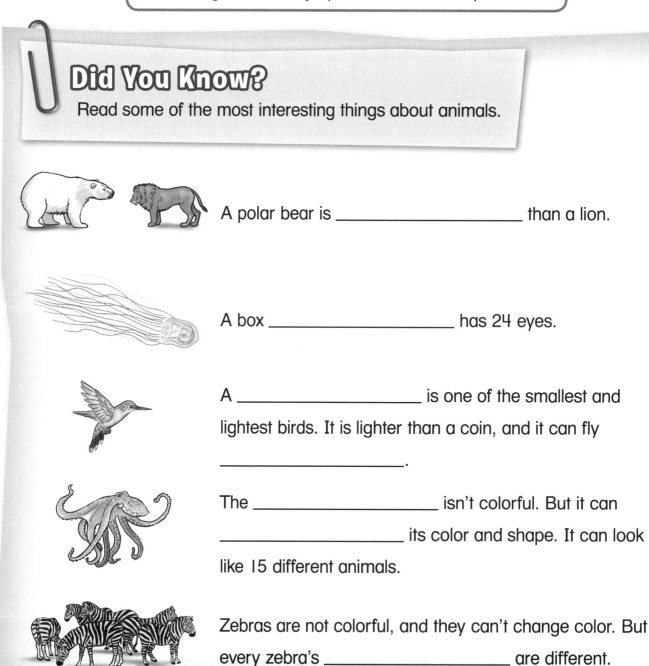

A polar bear is _____ than a lion.

A box _____ has 24 eyes.

A _____ is one of the smallest and lightest birds. It is lighter than a coin, and it can fly _____.

The _____ isn't colorful. But it can _____ its color and shape. It can look like 15 different animals.

Zebras are not colorful, and they can't change color. But every zebra's _____ are different.

B Answer the questions.

1. Which one is stronger, a lion or a polar bear?

   _____.

2. Are there a lot of eyes on a jellyfish?

   _____.

3. Which one is the lightest bird?

   _____.

4. What is the most interesting thing about a zebra?

   _____.

C Check the correct answer.

1. What does *backward* mean?

   A ☐    B ☐

2. A mimic octopus can change its shape. What does *change shape* mean?

   A ☐    B ☐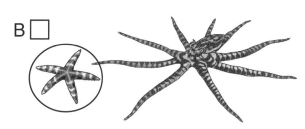

3. What do zebra stripes look like?

   A ☐    B ☐

D What about you? Answer the questions.

1. Which animal do like the best? _____

   _____.

2. What is interesting about your favorite animal? _____

   _____.

Let's Review

A Read and match.

1. Are there enough? ●   ● I didn't know that.
2. Are you sure? ●   ● I don't think so.
3. A cat is as fast as a polar bear. ●   ● Yes, I'm sure.
4. We don't have enough. ●   ● Are you sure? There are thee bags.

B Write the questions and answers.

1. _____ ?
   There's a lot of cheese.

2. _____ ?
   There are a few sandwiches.

3. How many cupcakes are there?

   _____ .

4. How much lemonade is there?

   _____ .

C Check the answer.

1. Which one is slower—the turtle or the gazelle?
   ☐ The turtle is slower.
   ☐ The gazelle is slower.

2. Which one is the largest—the elephant, the squirrel, or the wolf?
   ☐ The elephant is the largest.
   ☐ The squirrel is the largest.
   ☐ The wolf is the largest.

D Read and match.

Ni Hao from
Panda Kindergarten, China!

1. This week, we're volunteering at a panda kindergarten. Every morning, we clean the pandas' rooms, and then we feed them. They eat a lot of bamboo every day! Pandas also like carrots and apples. We didn't know that.

2. Newborn pandas are very small. They are about as light as a stick of butter. But they grow quickly.

3. We like watching the pandas. They really like to play. Baby pandas like to tumble, climb, and chase. They are very funny.

E True or false? Check the answer.

	TRUE	FALSE
1. Newborn pandas are large.		
2. Pandas eat a lot of bamboo.		
3. Pandas like carrots.		
4. Baby pandas like to climb.		
5. Newborn pandas grow slowly.		

Unit 3 Last Weekend

Let's Talk

A Read and write.

went for a bike ride   went shopping
weekend   pretty good   was
yours   did you do   Thanks

1. How was your _____?

   It _____ great.

   How was _____?

   It was _____.

2. What did you do?

   My brother and I _____

   _____.

   That sounds like fun.

3. What _____ on the weekend?

   I _____

   and bought this new bike.

   Wow! I like it.

   _____.

B Read and write.

It was great!   Wow! I like it.   Thanks!   That sounds like fun.

1. I bought a new bike.

   _____.

2. How was your weekend?

   _____!

3. I went skating.

   _____.

4. I like your bike.

   _____!

C Look, read, and write.

| went shopping | went skating | went for a swim | went bowling |

1.

What did he do last weekend?

He went _____.

2.

_____ last weekend?

They _____.

3.

_____ last weekend?

They _____.

4.

_____ last weekend?

She _____.

D What about you? Write.

What did you do on the weekend?

_____.

Let's Learn

A Unscramble, write, and match.

1. _____ •
   khiing

2. _____ •
   gkaint treisucp

3. _____ •
   kroadbaetsing

4. _____ •
   ylaipng allllboevy

5. _____ •
   gnrinnu

6. _____ •
   kliwang het ogds

B Look, read and check.

1.

What was she doing?
- [ ] She was hiking.
- [ ] She was walking the dogs.

2.

What was he doing?
- [ ] He was skateboarding.
- [ ] He was running.

C Write the questions and answers.

1.

What was he doing yesterday?

He was walking the dogs.

2.

What were they _____ ?

They were _____ .

3.

_____ ?

_____ .

4.

_____ ?

_____ .

5.

_____ ?

_____ .

6.

_____ ?

_____ .

Let's Learn More

A Match.

1. buying  the Internet

2. watching catch

3. playing  DVDs

4. borrowing  a package

5. mailing  books

6. surfing  sneakers

B Look at A. Write the words.

1. buying sneakers _____
2. _____
3. _____
4. _____
5. _____
6. _____

C Complete the sentences.

| at home | at the mall | at the library | at the post office |

1.

Where was he this afternoon?

He was _at the mall._

2.

Where were they this afternoon?

They were _____.

3.

Where _____?

_____.

4.

_____?

_____.

D Look at C. Answer the questions.

1. What was he doing?

   He was buying sneakers at the mall.

2. What were they doing?

   _____ at home.

3. What were they doing?

   _____.

4. What was she doing?

   _____.

Let's Read

A Read and write.

| jam | only | picking | ripe | row | seeds |

A Trip to the Strawberry Farm

Last weekend, I went to a strawberry farm with my family. We picked a lot of _____, red strawberries.

Strawberries are the _____ fruit with _____ on the outside.

I was picking strawberries in one row. My brother and my parents were in the next _____. I was watching my brother. Sometimes he was _____ strawberries, but usually he was eating them.

We took them home and made strawberry _____ and strawberry ice cream. It was fun!

B Answer the questions.

1. Where did they go last weekend?

_____.

2. What were they doing at the farm?

_____.

3. Who was eating the strawberries?

_____.

4. Are there a lot of fruits with seeds on the outside?

_____.

C Check the correct answer.

1. What does *ripe* mean?

A ☐

B ☐

2. Strawberries are the only fruit with seeds on the outside. What does *outside* mean?

A ☐

B ☐

3. What do *rows* look like?

A ☐

B ☐

D What about you?

1. What did you do last weekend? _____

_____.

2. What is your favorite jam? _____.

Let's Talk

A Unscramble and write.

1.

Are you ready?

Not yet. _____.

          minute   a   Wait

2.

Why?

_____.

to   forgot   something   I   I   think   do

3.

_____?

put   on   you   sunscreen   Did

Yes, I did. I put it on.

4.

_____?

off   you   radio   turn   the   Did

Yes, I turned it off.

5.

Now I remember.

_____.

I   take   off   watch   my   forgot   to

B Match.

1. turn in your homework •

•

2. turn up the heat •

3. turn down the music •

4. turn off the radio •

C Answer the questions.

1.

Did you clean up the room?

Yes, I cleaned it up.

2.

Did you take off your watch?

_____.

3.

Did you turn on the TV?

_____.

4.

Did you put on sunscreen?

_____.

Let's Learn

A Find, circle, and write the words.

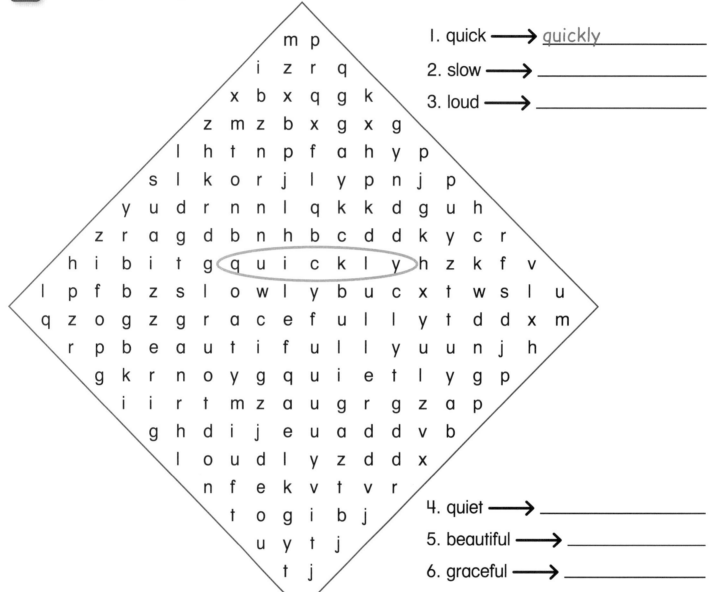

```
        m p
       i z r q
      x b x q g k
     z m z b x g x g
    l h t n p f a h y p
   s l k o r j l y p n j p
  y u d r n n l q k k d g u h
 z r a g d b n h b c d d k y c r
h i b i t g q u i c k l y h z k f v
l p f b z s l o w l y b u c x t w s l u
q z o g z g r a c e f u l l y t d d x m
 r p b e a u t i f u l l y u u n j h
  g k r n o y g q u i e t l y g p
   i i r t m z a u g r g z a p
    g h d i j e u a d d v b
     l o u d l y z d d x
      n f e k v t v r
       t o g i b j
        u y t j
         t j
```

1. quick ⟶ <u>quickly</u>

2. slow ⟶ _____

3. loud ⟶ _____

4. quiet ⟶ _____

5. beautiful ⟶ _____

6. graceful ⟶ _____

B Look, read, and circle.

1.

He speaks   quietly.
            loudly.

2.

He walks   quickly.
          slowly.

3.

She paints   gracefully.
           beautifully.

C Look and answer the questions.

Joe	Dan	Liz

1. Does Joe walk quickly?

   <u>Yes, he does.</u>

   Does he speak quietly?

   <u>No, he doesn't.</u>

   Does he paint beautifully?

   _____.

2. Does Dan walk quickly?

   _____.

   Does he speak quietly?

   _____.

   Does he paint beautifully?

   _____.

D Look at C. Write questions about Liz.

1. <u>Does she walk slowly?</u>

   Yes, she does.

2. _____?

   No, she doesn't.

3. _____?

   Yes, she does.

Let's Learn More

A Unscramble and write.

1. wse

_____

2. ookc

_____

3. ebka

_____

4. ylpa eht targiu

_____

Hello!

5. paesk gisElnh

_____

6. deri a cuinycel

_____

B Unscramble and write.

1. bakes / He / well / very

   He bakes very well. _____

2. cooks / well / She / very

   _____ .

3. very / She / well / sews

   _____ .

4. guitar / well / He / plays / very / the

   _____ .

C Look and write.

plays	cooks	dances	speaks	walks
well	gracefully	quickly	beautifully	loudly

1. He walks quickly.
2. _____.
3. _____.
4. _____.
5. _____.

D Read and draw.

He rides a skateboard very gracefully.

She plays the guitar very well.

A Read and write.

| hole | storm | swirl | tightly | tornado | wind |

A Tornado in a Bottle

A tornado is a _____. In this storm, the _____ moves very quickly in a circle. Tornadoes can pick up trees, cars, and houses!

You can make a model tornado in a bottle. Here's how to do it.

a. Use two bottles. Put water in one of the bottles. Put tape on the mouth of the bottle. Make a _____.

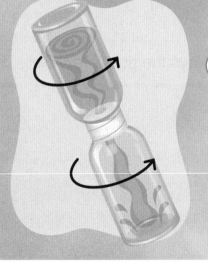

b. Tape the necks of the bottles _____ together. Turn over the bottles.

Tilt the bottles and _____ the water in a circle. You are going to see a little _____.

B Answer the questions.

1. How does the wind move in a tornado?

_____.

2. Are tornadoes very dangerous?

_____.

3. What can tornadoes pick up?

_____.

4. You want to make a tornado in a bottle. What do you need?

_____.

C Check the correct answer.

1. What does *tilt* mean?

A ☐

B ☐

2. What does *pick up* mean?

A ☐

B ☐

3. What does a *storm* look like?

A ☐

B ☐

D What about you?

1. Do you like stormy weather? _____.

2. What is your favorite kind of weather? _____

_____.

Let's Review

A Look and write.

1. Did you turn
down the music?

 _____
_____

2. Did you turn
on the TV?

 _____
_____

3. Did you clean
up your room?

<u>Yes, I turned</u>
<u>it down.</u>

4. Did you turn
up the heat?

_____
_____

B Write the questions and answers.

> put on sunscreen   eat quickly   ride slowly   play very well

1.

Did you _____ ?
No, I _____ .

2.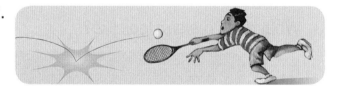

Did he _____ ?
_____ .

3.

Did she _____ ?
_____ .

4.

_____ ?
_____ .

C Read and write. Number the pictures.

> diving   Dolphins   reef   underwater

G'Day from the Great Barrier Reef in Australia

G'day from the Great Barrier Reef in Australia!

1. Today we went scuba _____. We swam slowly around the coral and saw some clownfish. They were very colorful and friendly.

2. Then we saw a big sea turtle. Turtles are not graceful on land, but they are very graceful in the water.

3. We swam back to the boat. _____ swam next to us and jumped out of the water.

4. This is the world's largest coral _____. It's a beautiful _____ world!

D True or false? Check the answer.

	TRUE	FALSE
1. There is coral in the Great Barrier Reef.		
2. Green turtles live on land and in water.		
3. Dolphins live on land and in water.		
4. Dolphins swim slowly.		
5. The coral reefs are very big.		

Let's Talk

A Look and number.

| | What about me? What do you think I'll be? | **1** | What do you want to be when you grow up? |

| | I think I'll be a designer. | | Really? I don't think so. I hate math. |

| | Good idea! You play tennis very well. | | You're probably right. You're good at drawing. |

| | I want to be a tennis player. | | Hmm. Maybe you'll be an engineer. |

B Look and write.

Across

1.

2.

hair stylist   movie director
designer   flight attendant
tennis player   surgeon

1. ___ ___ ___ ___ ___ | 4. ___ ___ ___ ___ | t ___ ___ ___ ___ ___

3. ___
   ___
   ___

2. ___ ___ ___ ___ ___ ___ ___ ___ ___

   d
   ___
   ___
   ___
   ___
   ___
   ___
   ___

5.
6. g

Down

3.

4.

5.

6.

Let's Learn

A Look at the chores. Answer the questions.

Kate's Chores This Week							
	Sunday	Monday	Tuesday	Wednesday	Thursday	Friday	Saturday
do the laundry							
set the table		✔		✔			
make the bed	✔	✔	✔	✔	✔	✔	✔
dust the furniture	✔						
mop the floor							
wash the car							✔

Scott's Chores This Week							
	Sunday	Monday	Tuesday	Wednesday	Thursday	Friday	Saturday
do the laundry	✔						
set the table							
make the bed	✔	✔	✔	✔	✔	✔	✔
dust the furniture	✔						
mop the floor			✔				
wash the car							

1. Will he make the bed?

   Yes, he will.

2. Will she mop the floor?

   No, she won't.

3. Will she make the bed?

   _____.

4. Will she wash the car?

   _____.

5. Will he dust the furniture?

   _____.

6. Will he set the table?

   _____.

7. Will he wash the car?

   _____.

8. Will she do the laundry?

   _____.

B Look and check. What will they probably do next?

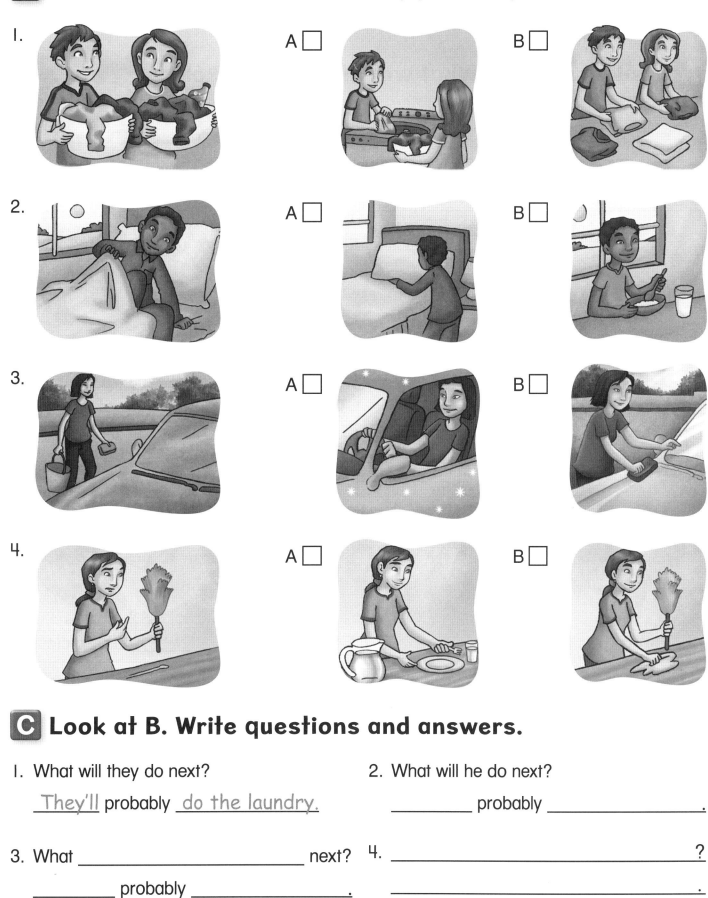

1. A ☐   B ☐

2. A ☐   B ☐

3. A ☐   B ☐

4. A ☐   B ☐

C Look at B. Write questions and answers.

1. What will they do next?

   They'll probably do the laundry.

2. What will he do next?

   _____ probably _____.

3. What _____ next?

   _____ probably _____.

4. _____?

   _____.

Let's Learn More

A Look and write. What will they do after class?

do homework	wash the dishes	go fishing
go swimming	go bowling	go to sleep

1. I think I'll <u>go fishing</u> after class.

2. I think I'll _____ after class.

3. I think I'll _____ after class.

4. I think I'll _____ after class.

5. _____.

6. _____.

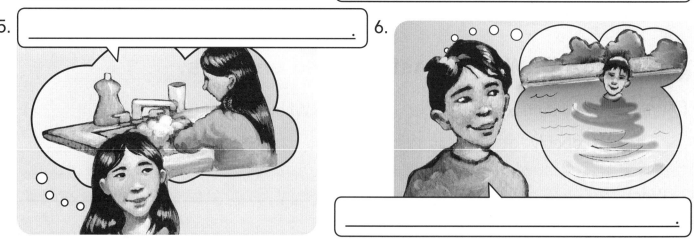

B Look, read, and circle. Check True or False.

1.

He'll
She'll   probably do homework.
They'll

☐ True   ☐ False

2.

He'll
She'll   probably go swimming.
They'll

☐ True   ☐ False

3.

He
She   probably won't go fishing.
They

☐ True   ☐ False

4.

He'll
She'll   probably go bowling.
They'll

☐ True   ☐ False

5.

He
She   probably won't clean the desk.
They

☐ True   ☐ False

6.

He
She   probably won't do homework.
They

☐ True   ☐ False

C What will you probably do next weekend?

_____.

A Put the story in order.

ELEPHANT CAMP

☐ Maybe they'll be soccer players or painters someday!

☐ Another elephant was painting a picture. Her name was Sai. She wrapped her trunk around the paintbrush. She painted a picture of an elephant. Sai can paint better than I can!

☐ Today I went to an elephant camp in Thailand. The elephants and their trainers were playing soccer! They were very good. The elephants can play soccer better than I can!

☐ I visited the elephant nursery, too. The baby elephants were very cute. They played all day.

B Answer the questions.

1. Where were the elephants?

_____

_____ .

2. What were the elephants doing?

a. _____ .

b. _____ .

c. _____ .

C Check the correct answer.

1. What is the *trunk* of an elephant?

A ☐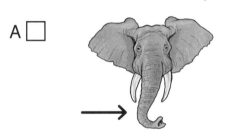

B ☐

2. What does *trainer* mean?

A ☐

B ☐

3. What does a *nursery* look like?

A ☐

B ☐

D What about you?

1. Do you like elephants? _____ .

2. What is your favorite animal? _____

_____ .

Let's Talk

A Look, read, and check.

1. What's your favorite season?
   Summer.
   Why?
   Because there's no school.

2. What's your favorite season?
   Winter.
   Why?
   Because I like skiing.

3. I like skiing too... waterskiing!
   That sounds like fun.

B Read and circle.

1. I like waterskiing.

   a. Good idea.   b. That sounds like fun.

2. What's your favorite season?
   Summer.

   a. I think so.   b. Why?

3. My favorite season is winter.

   a. Why?   b. Are you sure?

   Because I like skiing.

C Look, read, and write.

> skiing   planting flowers   picking apples   going to the beach

1. Why do you like summer?

   I like summer because I like _____

   _____.

2. Why do you like fall?

   _____

   _____.

3. _____ spring?

   _____

   _____.

4. _____ winter?

   _____

   _____.

D What about you? Write.

1. I like _____ because I like _____.

2. I don't like _____ because _____.

Let's Learn

A Match.

1.

raked leaves

2.

had a picnic

3.

picked flowers

4.

went sledding

5.

went backpacking

6.

built a sandcastle

B Look at the chart. Complete the questions and answers.

	Saturday	Sunday
Bill and Steve		
Jack		
June		
Debbie and Marie		

1. What did Bill and Steve do last weekend?

   They _had a snowball fight_ and they _went sledding._

2. What did Jack do last weekend?

   He _____, and he _____.

3. _____ last weekend?

   She _____, and she _____.

4. _____?

   _____, and they _____.

C What about you? Write.

1. What did you do last weekend?

   I _____.

2. What did your friends do last weekend?

   They _____.

Let's Learn More

A Find and circle the words. Then write.

1.  go <u>trekking</u>

2. go h_____
   r_____

3. go r_____

4. go s_____

5. go s_____
   d_____

6. go to a b_____
   g_____

7. go s_____

8.  go to a w_____
   p_____

```
f h n s p l e m y b q a d s e
h o r s e b a c k r i d i n g
e i a n h i p x m p k j n l u
s w g o c c d q f u h j i h z
u p c w e w a t e r p a r k y
r k t b f h p l b j o k n i g
f a b o r t p p o o q j u i i
i x b a s e b a l l g a m e q
n p y r u y o a r a f t i n g
g o o d b v i o r k e d o y k
e u c i d t r e k k i n g n h
f o p n a b x b f v f f q e s
a t x g o j c d n i v p r s g
b s m z u m e e r o u y q f p
s c u b a d i v i n g k f v t
```

B What about you? Write.

What will you do on your next vacation?

I'll probably _____.

C Answer the questions. Then draw.

1. What did he do last fall?

   He went apple picking.

What will he do next fall?

He'll probably go trekking.

2. What did she do last winter?

   _____ .

What will she do next winter?

_____ .

3. What did they do last spring?

   _____ .

What will they do next spring?

_____ .

4. What did he do last summer?

   _____ .

What will he do next summer?

_____ .

A Read and write.

| butterflies | north | spread | wings | south | wonderful |

The monarch butterflies are here in California!
They usually live in the north in the summer.
Every winter, they _____ their
_____ and fly _____ to
Mexico because they don't like the cold.

In the winter, the butterflies stop in California to rest. They are in all the trees. Winter is my favorite season because the butterflies are here. They are graceful, colorful and _____.

Monarch _____ are beautiful. They fill
the sky with orange and black spots when they fly.

In the spring, they will fly
_____ again
to Canada.

Answer the questions.

1. Where do monarch butterflies live in the summer?

   _____ .

2. Where do the butterflies live in the winter?

   _____ .

3. What will they do in the spring?

   _____ .

4. Monarch butterflies fly north in the spring. Why?

   _____ .

C Check the correct answer.

1. What do *spots* look like?

   A ☐ 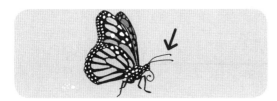   B ☐

2. "They fill the sky with orange and black spots." What does that mean?

   A ☐    B ☐

3. What does *fly north* mean?

   A ☐ 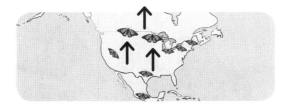   B ☐

D What about you?

1. Do you like butterflies? Why? _____

   _____ .

2. Do you live in the north or the south? _____ .

3. Is it cold in the winter there? _____ .

Let's Review ✓

A Write the questions and answers.

1. What do you think you'll be?

   _____ a tennis player.

2. What _____?
   I think she'll be a surgeon.

3. Why _____?
   I like winter because I like ice skating.

4. Why do you like spring?

   _____ flying kites.

B What about you? Write.

1. What's your favorite season? _____.

2. Why? _____.

C Look. Write the questions and answers.

1.

What did she do last winter?

_____.

What will she do next winter?

_____ probably _____.

2.

_____ summer?

They went trekking.

_____ summer?

They'll probably go camping.

D Read and write.

| climbers | delicious | friendly | guides | host family | season |

Namaste from Mt. Everest, Nepal

We're not at the top of Mt. Everest because only mountain _____ can go there. But we can see the top!

We stayed with a _____ in a small village last night. Everyone was very _____. We ate curry and bread for dinner. It was _____.

Summer is trekking _____. It's too cold in the winter. Tomorrow, our _____ will take us to the Everest Base Camp. We'll be at the top of the world!

E Write the answers.

1. They are not at the top of Mt. Everest. Why?

   _____.

2. What did they do last night?

   _____.

3. Summer is trekking season. Why?

   _____.

4. What will they do tomorrow?

   _____.

A Read and match.

1. Something smells good. What are you doing? •

2. Are they done? •

3. Oh, no. They don't look good. •

4. I don't know. Do you want one? •

5. How is it? •

• It tastes great!

• Almost.

• Sure.

• What happened?

• I'm baking cookies.

B Unscramble and write.

1.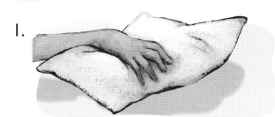

Touch the pillow.
cTuoh

It _feels_ soft.
lefes

2.

_____ the music.
stLine ot

It _____ wonderful.
sdsuon

3.

_____ the flower.
lemlS

It _____ good.
sllems

4.

_____ the strawberry.
estaT

It _____ sweet.
tsates

5.

_____ the butterfly.
koLo ta

It _____ beautiful.
skool

C Look and write.

| listen | look | smell | touch |

1. _____

2. _____

3. _____

4. _____

Let's Learn

A Unscramble and write. Then label.

looks   sounds   smells

1.

____bad____
bda

_____
dogo

____smells____

2.

_____
uflaw

_____
fonredwlu

_____

3.

_____
gluy

_____
ebaufitlu

_____

B Look at A. Write.

1. The skunk _smells bad_____.

2. The flower _____.

3. The music _____.

4. The music _____.

5. The house _____.

6. The house _____.

C Write the questions and answers.

1.

How does the music sound?

It _____ .

2.

How does the sunset look?

It _____ .

3.

How does the soap smell?

_____ .

4.

_____ ?

It smells good.

5.

_____ ?

It smells bad.

6.

_____ ?

It looks beautiful.

D What about you? Write.

1. How does your classroom look?

_____ .

2. How does your favorite food smell?

_____ .

3. How does your favorite music sound?

_____ .

Let's Learn More

A Write the words.

Feels	Tastes
hard	salty

salty	smooth
sour	bitter
hard	soft
rough	sweet

B Look at the pictures. Write sentences. Use the words in A.

1.
   The dark chocolate tastes bitter.

2.
   _____.

3.
   _____.

4.
   _____.

5.
   _____.

C Write the answers.

1.

Does the garbage smell good or bad?

It smells _____ .

2.

Does the bed feel hard or soft?

_____ .

3.

Does the music sound awful or wonderful?

_____ .

4.

Does the bird look ugly or beautiful?

_____ .

5.

Does the potato chip taste salty or sour?

_____ .

6.

Does the watermelon taste sweet or bitter?

_____ .

A Read and write.

| flavor | pinch | smell | taste buds | tongue |

Why Do Foods Taste Different?

You need two things to taste food: _____ and a sense of smell.

Taste buds are on your _____. They help you taste each kind of _____. Taste buds tell you that ice cream is sweet, potato chips are salty, lemons are sour, and some dark chocolate is bitter.

Your sense of _____ is important, too. It helps you taste..

Try this. Drink a glass of apple juice. It will taste sweet. Then _____ your nose closed. Drink some more juice. Now you can't taste it because you can't smell it.

Sweet

Sour

Bitter

Salty

B Answer the questions.

1. Where are taste buds?

_____.

2. What do taste buds help you do?

_____.

3. What other sense helps you taste?

_____.

4. Can you taste juice when you pinch your nose closed?

_____.

C Read and number the pictures.

1. Your sense of smell helps you taste.

2. Pinch your nose, and you can't smell or taste food.

3. Drink a glass of apple juice. It'll taste sweet.

4. Now pinch your nose closed and drink again. It has no taste.

D What about you? Answer the questions.

1. What's your favorite sweet food?

_____.

2. What's your favorite salty food?

_____.

A Look and number.

1.

☐ That's exciting!

☐ What?

1 Guess what!

☐ I'm going to France this summer.

2.

☐ No. It's my first time.

☐ Have you been there before?

☐ You'll love it.

☐ I've been there twice.

3.

☐ My uncle lives there.

☐ Wow!

☐ I visited him last summer.

☐ You're lucky.

B Match.

1.

• France

2.

• Egypt

3.

• Hawaii

4.

• China

5.

• Nepal

C Look. Complete the questions and answers.

1. Have you ever been to Hawaii?

No, _____.

2. Have you ever been to France?

Yes, _____.

3. _____ to China?

_____.

4. _____ to Egypt?

_____.

5. _____ to _____?

Yes, _____.

Let's Learn

A Find and circle the words.

fried noodles   crepes   potato salad   kimchi   sushi   tofu   ravioli   tacos

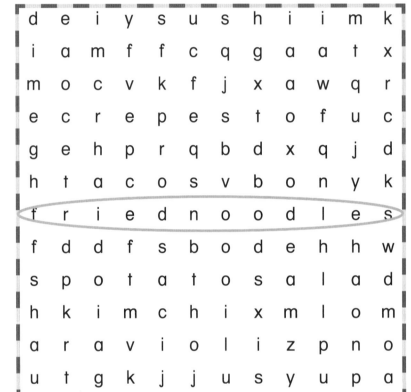

d	e	i	y	s	u	s	h	i	i	m	k
i	a	m	f	f	c	q	g	a	a	t	x
m	o	c	v	k	f	j	x	a	w	q	r
e	c	r	e	p	e	s	t	o	f	u	c
g	e	h	p	r	q	b	d	x	q	j	d
h	t	a	c	o	s	v	b	o	n	y	k
f	r	i	e	d	n	o	o	d	l	e	s
f	d	d	f	s	b	o	d	e	h	h	w
s	p	o	t	a	t	o	s	a	l	a	d
h	k	i	m	c	h	i	x	m	l	o	m
a	r	a	v	i	o	l	i	z	p	n	o
u	t	g	k	j	j	u	s	y	u	p	a

B What about you? Write.

1. Have you ever eaten fried noodles?

_____.

2. Have you ever eaten crepes?

_____.

C Look. Write the questions and answers.

1.

Have you ever eaten sushi?

Yes, <u>I have.</u>

<u>I've eaten sushi.</u>

2.

Have you ever eaten tofu?

No, _____.

<u>I've never eaten tofu.</u>

3.

Have you ever eaten kimchi?

Yes, _____.

_____.

4.

Have you ever eaten crepes?

No, _____.

_____.

5.

_____ ravioli?

Yes, _____.

_____.

6.

Have you ever eaten tacos?

_____ tacos?

No, _____.

_____.

Let's Learn More

A Look and number.

1. a crocodile   2. an ostrich   3. a panda   4. a penguin

5. a llama   6. a kangaroo   7. a koala   8. a hippopotamus

B What about you? Write.

1. Have you ever seen a koala?

_____.

2. Have you ever seen a cheetah?

_____.

C Read the chart. Write about Kate and Scott.

Has she ever...? Has he ever...?	Kate	Scott
...seen a kangaroo?	Yes	No
...eaten potato salad?	Yes	Yes
...been to the Great Barrier Reef?	No	No
...been to Hawaii?	No	Yes
...eaten fried noodles?	Yes	No
...seen a llama?	No	Yes

1. Has she ever seen a kangaroo?

   Yes, she has.

2. Has he ever seen a kangaroo?

   No, he hasn't.

3. Has she ever eaten potato salad?

   _____.

4. Has he ever been to the Great Barrier Reef?

   _____.

5. _____ Hawaii?

   Yes, _____.

6. _____ fried noodles?

   Yes, _____.

7. _____ llama?

   No, _____.

A Look, read, and put the steps in order.

The Dream Catcher

Do you ever have bad dreams at night?
Native Americans believe that a dream catcher can catch your unhappy dreams. Then you will only have happy dreams.
Have you ever seen a dream catcher? It looks like a spider's web.
You can make a dream catcher. Here is how to do it.

feathers   beads   a paper plate   yarn

[ ] Finally, tie feathers to the yarn.

[ ] Now weave across the plate. A few pieces of yarn can hang down. Put beads on the yarn.

[ ] Cut out the center of a paper plate. Around the plate, make holes about 1 cm apart.

[ ] Hang your dream catcher on the wall.

[ ] Put yarn into one hole. Then weave the yarn from hole to hole, up and over, around the plate.

[ ] Sweet dreams!

B Answer the questions.

1. What do Native Americans believe?

_____.

2. Where do you hang a dream catcher?

_____.

3. How many things do you need for a dream catcher?

_____.

4. What do you need to make a dream catcher?

_____.

C Check the correct answer.

1. What does a *spider's web* look like?

A ☐

B ☐

2. What does *weave* mean?

A ☐

B ☐

3. What does *hang down* mean?

A ☐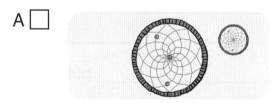

B ☐

D What about you?

1. Do you ever have bad dreams?

_____.

2. Do you want to make a dream catcher? What will you need?

_____

_____.

Let's Review

A Unscramble and write.

1. tastes chocolate dark bitter The

   _____ .

2. it feel smooth rough or Does

   _____ ?

3. the flower. Smell good It smells

   _____ .

4. eaten he ever Has tofu

   _____ ?

B What about you? Write the questions and answers.

1. <u>Have you ever been</u> to the Grand Canyon?

   _____ .

2. _____ to Australia?

   _____ .

3. _____ potato salad?

   _____ .

4. _____ a kangaroo?

   _____ .

5. _____ ravioli?

   _____ .

6. _____ a skunk?

   _____ .

C Read. Put the story in order.

Hello from the Grand Canyon, U.S.A.

☐ Tonight, we're going to sleep outside. We can hear the river. It sounds wonderful. We can also see a lot of stars. We've never seen so many stars!

☐ In the afternoon, we camped near the river. For dinner, the guides cooked steaks over a campfire. The steaks smelled and tasted delicious!

☐ *Hello* from the Grand Canyon, U.S.A.!

☐ This morning, we went rafting on the Colorado River. The river goes through the Grand Canyon. We went through a lot of rapids. They were very rough. We've never gone rafting before. It was exciting.

D Read the story again. Number the pictures.

E Read and check.

1. What happened?
   ☐ They went rafting.
   ☐ They went hiking.

2. What are they going to do?
   ☐ cook steaks outside
   ☐ sleep outside

3. What can they hear?
   ☐ the river
   ☐ the stars

Extra Practice

Let's Eat!

A Look and write questions and answers.

1. How much pizza is there?

   There is a lot.

2. How many sandwiches are there?

   _____ .

3. Are there a lot of pretzels?

   _____ .

4. How many pieces of watermelon are there?

   _____ .

5. Is there a lot of water?

   _____ .

6. Are there a lot of cookies?

   _____ .

7. _____ ?

   _____

Which Pet?

A Complete the sentences.

| graceful | beautiful | colorful | expensive | more | less |

$50.00

$35.00

1. The bird is _____ less graceful _____
   than the cat.

2. The cat is _____
   than the bird.

3. The cat is _____
   than the bird.

4. The bird is _____
   than the cat.

B What about you? Write.

1. My favorite animal is a _____.

2. I like it because it's _____.

3. I think a _____ is more _____ than a _____.

4. I think it's less _____ than a _____.

What Did You Do?

A Read and number.

1. They went for a walk.

2. She went shopping.

3. They went for a bike ride.

4. He went bowling.

B Complete the conversation.

1. Hi, Sue. Where were you yesterday?

2. _____ at the library.

3. Really? _____ library, too!

4. What were you _____?

5. I was studying. What _____ doing?

6. _____ borrowing books.

Activities

A Look and write the questions and answers.

	Rick	**Liz**
paint	beautifully	very well
walk	quickly	very slowly
speak	very loudly	very quietly
dance	very well	gracefully

1. Did Rick speak quietly?

   No, he didn't. He spoke very loudly.

2. Did he speak loudly?

   Yes, he did. He spoke very loudly.

3. Did Liz paint well?

   _____ .

4. Did Rick walk slowly?

   _____ .

5. Did Rick dance well?

   _____ .

6. Did Liz speak loudly?

   _____ .

7. _____ ?

   _____ .

My Future

A Read.

Maya is good at science. She thinks she'll be a scientist in the future. But she likes helping people, too. Maybe she'll be a surgeon. Maya likes clothes, too. Sometimes she thinks she'll be a fashion designer. She'll have an amazing future!

B What about you? Write.

I am good at _____ . I think I'll be _____

_____

_____

_____

_____

_____

_____

_____

_____ .

My Favorite Season

A Read. Write the seasons.

winter   spring   fall   summer

Gina

Favorite food: _oranges_

Favorite weather: _hot_

Favorite activity: _swimming_

Favorite season: _____

Dan

Favorite food: _salad_

Favorite weather: _warm_

Favorite activity: _planting flowers_

Favorite season: _____

Ellen

Favorite food: _hot chocolate_

Favorite weather: _cold_

Favorite activity: _skiing_

Favorite season: _____

Mark

Favorite food: _apples_

Favorite weather: _cool_

Favorite activity: _hiking_

Favorite season: _____

B What about you? Write.

1. My favorite food is _____.

2. My favorite weather is _____.

3. My favorite activity is _____.

4. My favorite season is _____.

✓ Parent's
signature: _____

Tacos and Crocodiles

A Read.

Sam: Guess what! I'm going to Mexico this summer.

Deb: Wow! You're lucky! Have you ever been there before?

Sam: No. It's my first time. Have you ever been to Mexico?

Deb: Yes, I have. I've been there twice. It was great!

Sam: That's exciting. I've never eaten tacos. And I've never seen a crocodile.

Deb: I've seen crocodiles. And I've eaten tacos. They were delicious!

B Answer the questions.

1. Has Deb ever eaten tacos? _____.

2. Has Sam ever eaten tacos? _____.

3. Has Sam ever been to Mexico? _____.

4. Has Deb ever seen a crocodile? _____.

C What about you? Write.

1. Have you ever seen a crocodile? _____.

2. Have you ever eaten tacos? _____.